교원임용시험 전공영어 대비 [제1판]

NEW

Build Up

박문각 임용

동영상강의 www.pmg.co.kr

박현수 영어교육론

III-2 기출문제

Guideline for Pre-service Teachers

나의 기출분석 및 오답분석

박문각

Contents

NEW

Build Up

Chapter
01

Second Language Acquisition - Theoretical Background

Second Language Acquisition – Theoretical Background

>> 모범답안 p.036

1 Teaching Methods & Approaches

01 **Read the conversation and follow the directions.** [2 points] 2022 전공A 2번

> T1 : Hello, Ms. Kim. You seem to be in deep thought. Anything bothering you?
>
> T2 : Good morning, Mr. Lee. I'm thinking of how to make my English class more effective.
>
> T1 : Yeah, I've been thinking about that, too.
>
> T2 : You know, our textbook is organized by separate language skills. But the four skills are rarely separable from each other, I think.
>
> T1 : True. Speaking almost always implies a listener, and writing and reading share obvious links.
>
> T2 : That's exactly what I mean.
>
> T1 : Actually, I've been adapting the textbook since last semester so that my students can be exposed to the language they will encounter in the real world.
>
> T2 : Sounds great. How have you been doing it?
>
> T1 : For example, I usually have pre-reading discussion time to activate schemata. It helps to make links between speaking, listening, and reading. My students actively engage in those kinds of tasks.
>
> T2 : That can be a good way. Or I could create a listening task accompanied by note-taking or followed by a group discussion.
>
> T1 : Great idea. I think just a slight change can make a big difference.
>
> T2 : Right. I'll try to make some changes and let you know how it goes. Thanks for sharing your experience!
>
> T=teacher

Fill in the blank with the ONE most appropriate word.

> In the above conversation, the two teachers are talking about the _____ approach, which is now typical within a communicative, interactive framework. The approach can give students greater motivation and make them engage more actively, which can convert to better learning outcomes.

Your Answer _____

기입형 Worksheet

Topic/나의 점수/ 정답률	감점 원인 분석 및 수정전략	Topic-related Key Terms & Concepts & Phrases
	(1) 감점 원인 분석 (2) 수정 및 정리 전략 (mapping)	

02 **Read the dialogue and follow the directions.** [2 points] 2018 전공A 7번

(A teacher and a student are talking after seeing a video-clip of a baseball game.)

T: What was happening in the video?
S: A ball, uh, a ball.
T: A ball was thrown.
S: Thrown?
T: Yes, thrown. A ball was thrown.
S: A ball thrown.
T: And who threw the ball?
S: Pitcher. Thrown pitcher.
T: Thrown by the pitcher.
S: By pitcher.
T: Yes, by the pitcher. A ball was thrown by the pitcher.
S: Ball thrown by pitcher.

T=teacher, S=student

Fill in the blank with the FOUR most appropriate words.

From a socio-cultural perspective, effective learning takes place when what a student attempts to learn is within his or her _____.
This is the distance between what a student can do alone and what he or she can do with scaffolded help from more knowledgeable others like teachers or more capable peers. For learning to be effective, such help should be provided to a student through interaction like the teacher's utterances offered to aid the student in the above dialogue.

(Your Answer) _____

기입형 Worksheet

Topic/나의 점수/ 정답률	감점 원인 분석 및 수정전략	Topic-related Key Terms & Concepts & Phrases
	(1) 감점 원인 분석 (2) 수정 및 정리 전략 (mapping)	

2 Interlanguage Development

01 Read the passage in <A> and the interaction in <B>, and follow the directions. [4 points] 2021 전공B 7번

A

Some studies claim that there is a predictable language development. For instance, the following is one way of understanding developmental stages for question formation, which posits six stages, each with some prominent features.

Stage	Key Feature	Example
1	• Rising intonation on word or phrase	*Airplane?*
2	• Rising intonation with a declarative word order	*You like this?*
3	• Fronting (e.g., *do*-fronting, *wh*-fronting, other fronting)	*Where the train is going?* *Is the boy has a dog?*
4	• Inversion in *wh*-questions with a copula *be* • No inversion in *wh*-questions with auxiliaries • Yes/no questions with auxiliaries such as *can* and *will*	*Where is the book?* *Where I can draw them?* *Can he catch the ball?*
5	• Inversion in *wh*-questions with both an auxiliary and a copula *be*	*How can she solve it?*
6	• Complex questions (e.g., tag questions, embedded questions)	*She's pretty, isn't she?* *Can you tell me where he is?*

The information about the sequences in English language acquisition like the above is mostly from child native speakers. Familiarity with them can help EFL teachers estimate their students' level of development, which in turn can help determine realistic goals for language instruction.

B

(Two students are doing an information-gap activity where they are supposed to spot the differences between two pictures.)

S1 : I see a dog in the middle.

S2 : Me, too.

S1 : Is the girl kicks a ball?

S2 : The boy kicks a ball in my picture. Where you can see the duck?

S1 : In the pond.

S2 : I can see the duck in the pond, too.

S1 : Is the boy flies kite?

S2 : No, the girl flies kite. Where are the birds?

S1 : In the trees.

S2 : I find birds on the tree, too.

S=student

Based on <A>, identify the developmental stages where S1 and S2 are, respectively, with evidence from <B>.

First Draft

_____

_____

_____

_____

_____

Revised Version

_____

_____

_____

_____

_____

서술형 Worksheet

Topic/나의 점수/ 오답분석 및 채점기준	수정 전략 및 주제관련 정리(mapping)	Topic-related Key Terms & Concepts & Phrases
(1) Topic/나의 점수/정답률		
(2) Directions Analysis		
(3) Data Processing		

3 Learning Phenomenon

01 **Read the interaction between a teacher and a student, and follow the directions.** [2 points] 2014 전공A 기입형 8번

> *(The teacher asks her student, Dongho, what he did over the weekend.)*
>
> T: Hi, Dongho, how was your weekend?
> S: Hello, uh, have, had fun.
> T: You had fun, oh, good. Did you go anywhere?
> S: Yeah, uh, I go, go, went to uncle, uncle's home.
> T: What did you do there? Did you do something interesting?
> S: I play, played with childs. Uncle have childs, three childs.
> T: Your uncle has three children?
> S: Yeah, uh, one boy and two girls. So three childs.
> T: Do you like them?
> S: Yeah. They're fun. They're good to me.
>
> T=teacher, S=student

Complete the comments on the interaction by filling in the blank with ONE word.

> Language errors may occur as a result of discrepancies between the learner's interlanguage and the target language. One main source of such errors is called _____, one example of which is seen in the student's use of *childs* in the given interaction.

(Your Answer) _____

기입형 Worksheet

Topic/나의 점수/ 정답률	감점 원인 분석 및 수정전략	Topic-related Key Terms & Concepts & Phrases
	(1) 감점 원인 분석 (2) 수정 및 정리 전략 (mapping)	

4 Discourse Structures & Negotiation Strategies

01 Read the passage in <A> and the conversation in <B>, and follow the directions. [3 points] 2014 전공A 서술형 2번

A

A typical conversation organized around making requests has a common overarching sequence of interactional moves:

• A greeting exchange
• Preliminary moves toward a forthcoming request
• Making the request
• Short negotiation about the request
• Acceptance/Rejection of the request
• Closing/Thanking

B

(*A low-proficiency English learner asks her roommate, a native speaker of English, to go buy some bread for her.*)

Jisu : Hi, Kelly.
Kelly : Hi, Jisu.
Jisu : Buy me bread, OK?
Kelly : Do you want bread?
Jisu : Yeah.
Kelly : So, there's no bread in the fridge?
Jisu : Sorry?
Kelly : You don't have bread?
Jisu : No.
Kelly : So, do you want me to go to the supermarket and get some bread for you?
Jisu : What was that?
Kelly : Do you want me to get bread for you?
Jisu : Yeah.
Kelly : Do you want it right now?

01

Jisu : Tomorrow morning.
Kelly : OK. I'll get it for you later tonight.
Jisu : OK. Thank you.

> Jisu=low-proficiency learner, Kelly=native speaker of English

Explain how the conversation in <B> deviates from the sequence of interactional moves in <A>. Then identify the strategy that Jisu uses when she does not understand Kelly.

First Draft

_____

_____

_____

_____

_____

_____

_____

_____

Revised Version

_____

_____

_____

_____

_____

_____

_____

_____

서술형 Worksheet

Topic/나의 점수/ 오답분석 및 채점기준	수정 전략 및 주제관련 정리(mapping)	Topic-related Key Terms & Concepts & Phrases
(1) Topic/나의 점수/정답률		
(2) Directions Analysis		
(3) Data Processing		

02 **Read the passage in <A> and the interaction in <B>, and follow the directions.** [4 points] 2021 전공A 10번

| A |

In language directed toward linguistically nonproficient second language speakers, native speakers tend to show foreigner-talk adjustments in the flow of conversation. These include slow speech rate, loud speech, long pauses, simple vocabulary (e.g., few idioms, high-frequency words), and paucity of slang. They also tend to make adjustments to their speech in the area of grammar. They often move topics to the front of the sentence, put new information at the end of the sentence, use fewer contractions and pronouns, grammatically repeat non-native speakers' incorrect utterances, and fill in the blank for their incomplete utterances.

| B |

NS : So what did you have for lunch today?

NNS : I was busy. I eated cookies.

NS : Oh, did you? I see.

NNS : You want cookies?

NS : No, thanks.

NNS : You don't like cookies?

NS : Well... these days I'm on a diet and I rarely eat them.

NNS : Sorry... I don't understand.

NS : These days I am on a diet and I rarely eat cookies.

NNS : Oh, I see. You diet. You don't eat cookies.

NS : Well, I do. But only sometimes.

NNS : Mm.... Sometime. You eat cookies only sometimes.

NS : Right, because they have too much sugar.

NS=native speaker, NNS=non-native speaker

Based on <A>, locate ONE utterance in <B> that reflects NS's grammatical adjustment to his speech and identify its adjustment type. Then, explain how it functions in the given dialogue.

First Draft

_____

_____

_____

_____

_____

_____

_____

_____

Revised Version

_____

_____

_____

_____

_____

_____

_____

_____

01

서술형 Worksheet

Topic/나의 점수/ 오답분석 및 채점기준	수정 전략 및 주제관련 정리(mapping)	Topic-related Key Terms & Concepts & Phrases
(1) Topic/나의 점수/정답률		
(2) Directions Analysis		
(3) Data Processing		

03 **Read the passages and follow the directions.** [4 points] 2017 전공B 4번

| A |

Meaning-negotiation strategies such as comprehension checks, clarification requests, and confirmation checks may aid comprehension during conversational interaction. First, comprehension checks are defined as the moves by which one interlocutor seeks to make sure that the other has understood correctly. Second, clarification requests are the moves by which one interlocutor requests assistance in understanding the other's preceding utterance. Finally, confirmation checks refer to the moves used by one interlocutor to confirm whether he or she correctly has understood what the other has said.

| B |

Miss Jeong has been instructing her students to actively utilize meaning-negotiation strategies stated in <A> during speaking activities. One day, she interviewed two of her students, Mijin and Haerim, about the strategies that they had used during previous speaking activities. The following are excerpts from the interview:

Mijin : When I didn't understand what my friends said during speaking activities, I usually said, "Could you repeat what you said?" or "I am sorry?" Sometimes I tried to check whether my friends clearly understood what I said by saying, "You know what I mean?"

Haerim : Well, during speaking activities, when I had difficulties comprehending what my friends said, I didn't say anything and pretended to understand what they said. I felt it embarrassing to show my lack of understanding to my friends. However, when I talked about something during speaking activities, I often said, "Do you understand?" in order to see if my utterances were understood well by my friends.

Based on the passage in <A>, write down all the meaning-negotiation strategies that Mijin and Haerim used respectively, along with their corresponding utterances from each student in <B>.

First Draft

_____

_____

_____

_____

_____

_____

_____

Revised Version

_____

_____

_____

_____

_____

_____

_____

_____

서술형 Worksheet

Topic/나의 점수/ 오답분석 및 채점기준	수정 전략 및 주제관련 정리(mapping)	Topic-related Key Terms & Concepts & Phrases
(1) Topic/나의 점수/정답률		
(2) Directions Analysis		
(3) Data Processing		

5　Cultural Learning

01　Read the teacher's note in <A> and the lesson plan in <B>, and follow the directions. [4 points] 2021 전공B 8번

A

Teacher's Note

  Last week, I attended a teacher training workshop on intercultural education. In the workshop, the trainer defined culture as the beliefs, way of life, art, and customs that are shared and accepted by people in a particular society. She also explained that understanding another culture involves constructing a new frame of reference in terms of the people who created it. I totally agree with her. I believe that in order to help my students develop intercultural competence, I need to have them understand their own frame of reference as well as the target culture's. I also think that it is necessary to utilize various materials to arouse students' interests. Below is the list of instructional techniques that the trainer taught us in the workshop.

• **Artifact study** : It is designed to help students discern the cultural significance of certain unfamiliar objects from the target culture. The activity involves students in giving descriptions and forming hypotheses about the function of the unknown object.

• **Culture capsule** : It is a brief description, usually one or two paragraphs, of some aspect of the target culture, followed by or incorporated with contrasting information about the students' native culture. Culture capsules can be written by teachers or students.

• **Culture island** : A culture island is an area in the classroom where posters, maps, objects, and pictures of people, lifestyles, or customs of other cultures are displayed to attract learners' attention, evoke comments, and help students develop a mental image.

• **Native informant** : Native informants can be valuable resources to the classroom teacher, both as sources of current information about the target culture and as linguistic models for students. Students can develop a set of questions they would like to ask before native speakers come to the class.

B

Lesson Plan

Unit 7 Hello From Around The World

Period 10th out of 12 sessions

Topic   Greeting customs in the UK

Goal   To teach about the ways in which people greet each other in the UK and how they are different from those in Korea

Preparation

Decorate the culture board in the English classroom with pictures and posters which illustrate the greeting customs of the UK.

Lesson Steps

1. Have the students check out the culture board and tell what they think about the pictures and posters.
2. Read aloud a short passage about greeting customs in the UK, which is prepared in advance, and have the students take notes.
3. Divide the students into small groups to compare their notes. Then, have them discuss and write the similarities and differences between Korea and the UK regarding the greeting customs.
4. Have the students imagine situations in which people from the two cultures meet. Ask them to write a conversation script based on the situation and to perform role-plays.

01

Based on <A>, identify TWO instructional techniques that the teacher implements in the lesson plan, with corresponding evidence from <B>.

First Draft

_____

_____

_____

_____

_____

_____

_____

Revised Version

_____

_____

_____

_____

_____

_____

_____

서술형 Worksheet

Topic/나의 점수/ 오답분석 및 채점기준	수정 전략 및 주제관련 정리(mapping)	Topic-related Key Terms & Concepts & Phrases
(1) Topic/나의 점수/정답률		
(2) Directions Analysis		
(3) Data Processing		

02 Read the passage in <A> and the lesson plan in <B>, and follow the directions. [4 points] 2023 전공A 12번

A

In designing activities for cultural instruction, it is important to consider the purpose of the activity, as well as its usefulness for teaching language and culture in an integrative fashion. The most basic issue in cross-cultural education is increasing the degree to which language and culture are integrated. Several suggestions for dealing with this issue are as follows:

1. Use cultural information when teaching vocabulary. Teach students about the cultural connotations of new words.
2. Present cultural topics in conjunction with closely related grammatical features whenever possible. Use cultural contexts for language-practice activities, including those that focus on particular grammatical forms.
3. Make good use of textbook illustrations or photos. Use probing questions to help students describe the cultural features of the illustrations or photos.
4. In group activities, use communication techniques for cultural instruction, such as discussions and role-plays.
5. Teach culture while involving the integration of the four language skills. Do not limit cultural instruction to lecture or anecdotal formats.

B

	Lesson 4. World-famous Holidays	
Objectives	Students will be able to 1. introduce world-famous holidays using *-er than* and 2. perform activities related to the holidays to deepen their understanding of diverse cultures.	
Development	Step 1	• T asks Ss to speak out about anything related to the pictures in the textbook on p. 78. • T asks Ss some questions to elicit their ideas about what cultural features they see in the pictures of world-famous holidays. • Ss tell each other about the cultural differences among the holidays based on the pictures.
	Step 2	• T tells Ss about the origins of the world-famous holidays in detail. • T explains the cultural characteristics of those holidays. • T shares his experiences related to the holidays, and Ss listen to T's stories.
	Step 3	• T has Ss listen to a story about the world-famous holidays, and underline the expressions of comparative forms in the story on p. 79. • T talks with Ss about the meanings and functions of the expressions based on the cultural characteristics of the holidays. • T asks Ss, in pairs, to search the Internet for more information about cultural differences among the holidays and to describe the differences using comparative forms.
	Step 4	• T introduces new words in the story on the screen. • T explains the meanings of the words (traditional, adapting, polite, etc.), comparing them with their synonyms and/or antonyms. • Ss note the words and memorize them using mnemonic devices.

Step 5	• T has Ss sit in groups of four, and choose one distinct aspect of the world-famous holidays, such as costume, food, and festivals. • Ss write a culture capsule in groups about the differences. • T gives preparation time, and each group performs a role-play based on the culture capsule in front of their classmates.

T=teacher, Ss=students

Identify the **TWO** steps from <B> that do **NOT** correspond to the suggestions in <A>. Then, support your answers, respectively, with evidence from <A> and <B>.

First Draft

_____

_____

_____

_____

_____

_____

Revised Version

_____

_____

_____

_____

_____

_____

서술형 Worksheet

Topic/나의 점수/ 오답분석 및 채점기준	수정 전략 및 주제관련 정리(mapping)	Topic-related Key Terms & Concepts & Phrases
(1) Topic/나의 점수/정답률		
(2) Directions Analysis		
(3) Data Processing		

Memo

01 · Second Language Acquisition-Theoretical Background

1 Teaching Methods & Approaches

01 integrated

02 zone of proximal development

2 Interlanguage Development

01 S1 belongs to the developmental stage 3, while S2 has key features of stage 4. In the conversation in <B>, S1 shows fronting saying "Is the girl kicks a ball?" and "Is the boy flies kite?". On the other hand, S2 says "Where you can see the duck?" and "Where are the birds?" in <B>, which reflects no inversion in *wh*-questions with auxiliaries, and inversion in *wh*-questions with copula *be*, respectively.

3 Learning Phenomenon

01 overgeneralization

4 Discourse Structures & Negotiation Strategies

01 The conversation in <B> omits "the preliminary moves toward a forthcoming request" from the sequence in <A>. Jisu simply greets Kelly and immediately makes the request of buying some bread for her. Also, when Jisu has trouble understanding Kelly, she uses a clarification request, as shown in her responses like "Sorry?" and "What was that?".

02 As a grammatical adjustment, NS says "These days I am on a diet and I rarely eat cookies." Compared to her/his earlier utterance, she/he uses fewer contractions and pronouns, which helps the NNS better understand the message by making its structure clearer.

03 Mijin uses both clarification requests and comprehension checks. She asks for clarification with expressions like "Could you repeat what you said?" or "I am sorry?" and checks comprehension by saying "You know what I mean?". Haerim uses a comprehension check only, as shown in her utterance "Do you understand?".

5 Cultural Learning

01 The first instructional technique the teacher uses is "Culture island," by decorating the culture board with posters and pictures related to UK greeting customs. The second technique is "Culture capsule," as students are asked to read about greeting customs in the UK and then compare them with Korean customs by writing similarities and differences.

02 Steps 2 and 4 do not follow suggestions 5 and 1, respectively. In Step 2, the teacher asks students to just listen to his/her experiences (anecdotes) and explanation (lecture) about world-famous holidays, not facilitating integrated skills. Also, in Step 4, without mentioning the cultural connotations of new words, the teacher just explains their meanings with synonyms and/or antonyms.

NEW

Build Up

Chapter
02

Classroom Contexts

Classroom Contexts

≫ 모범답안 p.066

1 Learner Variables

01 Read the questionnaire in <A> and the teacher's note in <B>, and follow the directions. [2 points] 2019 전공A 1번

| | A | |

This questionnaire is designed to identify students' learning styles. Each category (A, B, C, D) has 10 items. Students are asked to read each item and check their preferences.

	Learning Style Questionnaire	4	3	2	1
A	1. I understand better when I hear instructions.				
	2. I remember information better when I listen to lectures than when I read books.				
	3. I like to listen to radio shows and discussions more than reading the newspaper.				
	⋮				
B	1. I like to look at graphs, images, and pictures when I study.				
	2. I follow directions better when the teacher writes them on the board.				
	3. I can easily understand information on a map.				
	⋮				
C	1. I enjoy working with my hands or making things.				
	2. I remember things better when I build models or do projects.				
	3. I like to 'finger spell' when I learn words.				
	⋮				

D	1. I like activities that involve moving around.				
	2. I prefer to learn by doing something active.				
	3. I learn the best when I go on field trips.				
	⋮				

4=strongly agree, 3=agree, 2=disagree, 1=strongly disagree

B

Based on the findings of the questionnaire conducted in my class, I have noticed that four students each have a major learning style.

Scores of the four students

Youngmi	Minsu	Taeho	Suji
A = 38	A = 18	A = 15	A = 13
B = 11	B = 36	B = 12	B = 14
C = 10	C = 10	C = 40	C = 12
D = 12	D = 12	D = 11	D = 36

This week, I am going to teach names of wild animals, like 'ostrich' and 'rhinoceros,' by trying different activities to address these students' different learning styles. Youngmi scored the highest in category A, showing that she is an auditory learner. So I will let her listen to a recording and say the names of animals out loud. Minsu's high score in category B shows that he is a visual learner. I will let him look at images of animals and read the corresponding names. The person who had the highest score in C was Taeho, who is a tactile learner. I am going to use origami so he can use his hands to fold papers into animal shapes. This will help him learn their names better. Lastly, Suji's score in category D shows that she is a(n) _____ learner. For her, I am planning to do an animal charade activity where she acts like different animals and others guess the names of them. I think she will enjoy moving around the classroom. In these ways, I want to maximize students' learning outcomes in my class.

Based on the information in <A> and <B>, fill in the blank in <B> with the ONE most appropriate word.

Your Answer _____

02

기입형 Worksheet

Topic/나의 점수/ 정답률	감점 원인 분석 및 수정전략	Topic-related Key Terms & Concepts & Phrases
	(1) 감점 원인 분석 (2) 수정 및 정리 전략 (mapping)	

02 Read the passages and follow the directions. [4 points] 2019 전공B 4번

| A |

(Below is a student's writing and a conversation with his teacher about the writing.)

Student writing

> Someone first showed the bicycle to the public in the late 18th century. People first thought it was not safe or comfortable. But many creative people improved it. So, many people use the bicycle widely as a form of transportation or for exercise today. Bicycle makers manufacture lighter, faster and stronger bicycles now than before. Because of that, more people ride the bicycle around the world these days than any time in the past. But they used some unique types of cycles in the old days like the four-cycle.

Teacher-student one-on-one conference

T : What is this writing about?

S : It's about the bicycle. Do you ride a bicycle?

T : Yes, I sometimes do. So your writing is not about people who produce or use the bicycle.

S : That's right.

T : OK, the main theme is the bicycle. But none of the sentences has the bicycle as its subject.

S : I know. But if the bicycle becomes the subject, then I have to use many passives. They are complicated and difficult. So I tried not to use them.

T : But it would be better to use the bicycle as the subject in most sentences. That way, it will become clear that the main focus of your writing is the bicycle.

S : Well, okay. I'll try.

T : You used the word "manufacture." Did you know this word?

S : No, I didn't. At first, I wanted to use "make" but then the sentence looked a bit awkward because the subject is "makers." It would go like "Bicycle makers make."

T : I see.

S : So I looked up a different word in a dictionary that has the same meaning as "make."

T : That works. What about this word "four-cycle?" What do you mean? Are you trying to describe a bicycle but with four wheels?

S : Yes, I am. I added "four" to "cycle" just like "bi" is put before "cycle" in bicycle.

T : Oh, it is called "quadricycle." "Quadri" means four just as "bi" means two.

T=teacher, S=student

B

When writing as well as speaking in a second language, learners who have limited command of the second language may have to use a variety of strategies that can compensate for their lack of knowledge of the target language grammar and vocabulary in order to effectively get their intended meaning or message across to a reader or listener. Strategies employed for this purpose include avoidance, code switching, word coinage, appeal to authority, and using prefabricated patterns. As these strategies constitute a significant part of strategic competence, advances in the learners' ability to effectively use them play a considerable role in promoting their communicative competence.

Based upon the student's writing and his dialogue with the teacher in <A>, identify THREE strategies the student used from those mentioned in <B>. Then, provide corresponding evidence for each identified strategy from <A>.

First Draft

_____
_____
_____
_____
_____
_____
_____

Revised Version

_____
_____
_____
_____
_____
_____
_____

서술형 Worksheet

Topic/나의 점수/ 오답분석 및 채점기준	수정 전략 및 주제관련 정리(mapping)	Topic-related Key Terms & Concepts & Phrases
(1) Topic/나의 점수/정답률		
(2) Directions Analysis		
(3) Data Processing		

02

2 Classroom Management

01　**Read the passages and follow the directions.** [4 points] 2018 전공A 10번

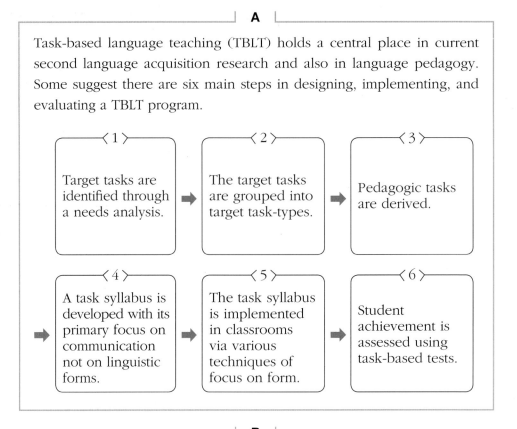

| A |

Task-based language teaching (TBLT) holds a central place in current second language acquisition research and also in language pedagogy. Some suggest there are six main steps in designing, implementing, and evaluating a TBLT program.

⟨1⟩
Target tasks are identified through a needs analysis.

⟨2⟩
The target tasks are grouped into target task-types.

⟨3⟩
Pedagogic tasks are derived.

⟨4⟩
A task syllabus is developed with its primary focus on communication not on linguistic forms.

⟨5⟩
The task syllabus is implemented in classrooms via various techniques of focus on form.

⟨6⟩
Student achievement is assessed using task-based tests.

| B |

Mr. Kim designed and implemented a TBLT program based on the six steps described in <A>.

- **Step 1.** He did some questionnaire surveys with his students and interviewed fellow teachers to identify what his students would really want to do in everyday life.

- **Step 2.** He grouped the identified real-world tasks (e.g., purchasing a train ticket, booking a room, renting a car) into more general categories (e.g., planning a trip).

> **· Step 3.** He developed tasks that his students would perform in the classroom. Those tasks were expected to elicit communicative language use in the classroom.
>
> **· Step 4.** He designed a syllabus with a central aim of presenting different grammatical items one at a time and teaching them separately.
>
> **· Step 5.** He drew student attention to linguistic forms when needed, while the primary focus of the lessons was still on communication during task performance.
>
> **· Step 6.** He assessed the student outcomes, focusing on whether and how much they accomplished each given task.

Identify the step in <B> that does not match with its corresponding suggestion in <A>. Then, explain how that identified step deviates from its suggestion in <A>. Do NOT copy more than FOUR consecutive words from the passage.

First Draft
_____
_____
_____
_____
_____

Revised Version
_____
_____
_____
_____
_____

서술형 Worksheet

Topic/나의 점수/ 오답분석 및 채점기준	수정 전략 및 주제관련 정리(mapping)	Topic-related Key Terms & Concepts & Phrases
(1) Topic/나의 점수/정답률		
(2) Directions Analysis		
(3) Data Processing		

02 Read the passage in <A> and the teaching procedure in <B>, and follow the directions. [4 points] 2021 전공A 9번

A

Mr. Yang, a middle school English teacher, believes that his lessons should help students meet the achievement standards which are specified in the school curriculum. He selects a group of standards for each semester and tries to incorporate them into his lessons. The following are the achievement standards for this semester.

Achievement Standards

[Oral Language Skills]

Students can
- use strategies to open and close conversations.
- explain their likes and dislikes.
- describe their dreams and future jobs.
- talk about their worries and problems.

[Written Language Skills]

Students can
- read a book or watch a film and write their feelings and impressions.
- read a short text about a familiar topic and write a conclusion.
- read a short text about a familiar topic and organize the content.
- view an object or picture and write their thoughts or feelings about it.

| **B** |

Teaching Procedure

Mr. Yang designed a reading lesson for his 2nd year students based on two of the achievement standards that he set out to accomplish this semester.

<Reading text>

What Should I Do?

Everyone has worries. When you have things you worry about, what do you do?

Sumi's Worries

Sumi thought Kate was her best friend, but now, she feels that Kate has changed and that she is avoiding her. A few days ago, Sumi met Kate in the hallway at school, but Kate turned around and walked away from her. Sumi tried to find the reason, but she couldn't think of anything wrong she had done to Kate. So, Sumi asked for her older sister's advice. Sumi's sister suggested that she simply ask Kate what's wrong.

Step 1	T tells Ss about today's topic and has Ss predict the content of the reading text based on the titles and pictures.
Step 2	T introduces new words from the text.
Step 3	T asks Ss to skim the text and tell what the text is about.
Step 4	T has Ss reread the text and complete a problem-solution chart based on what they read.
Step 5	T has Ss tell their worries and suggest solutions in groups.
Step 6	T has Ss write the key words and sentences in their learning log.

T=teacher, S=student

Identify ONE oral language achievement standard and ONE written language achievement standard from <A> that the teaching procedure in <B> targets. Then, explain how each achievement standard is addressed with evidence from <B>.

First Draft

_____

_____

_____

_____

_____

_____

_____

Revised Version

_____

_____

_____

_____

_____

_____

서술형 Worksheet

Topic/나의 점수/ 오답분석 및 채점기준	수정 전략 및 주제관련 정리(mapping)	Topic-related Key Terms & Concepts & Phrases
(1) Topic/나의 점수/정답률		
(2) Directions Analysis		
(3) Data Processing		

3 Textbook Evaluation and Adaptation, and Instruction Tools

01 Read the passages in <A> and <B>, and follow the directions. [4 points]

A

There are always sound reasons for adapting materials in order to make them as accessible and useful to learners as possible. When adapting materials, having clear objectives is a necessary starting point. The objectives a teacher may hope to achieve by adapting classroom materials can be listed as follows:

- To cater to learners' language proficiency levels: The teacher can modify the difficulty of language features such as grammar and vocabulary in the materials.
- To reinforce learner autonomy: Through materials adaptation, the teacher can give students opportunities to focus on their own learning processes to become more independent learners.
- To enhance higher-level cognitive skills: The teacher can adapt materials in such a way as to require students to hypothesize, predict, or infer.
- To encourage learners to tap into their own lives: Through materials adaptation, the teacher can increase the relevance of the contents or activities in relation to the students' experiences.

B

Ms. Lee is teaching first-year high school students, and she is preparing for her English reading class next semester. Based on the results of a needs analysis, she has decided to adapt two chapters of the textbook materials to meet her students' needs. For Lesson 2, which is about career paths, she will use magazine pictures of various jobs like engineer, baker, and fashion designer, along with some pictures related to jobs in the textbook. She will use these pictures as a springboard to get students in groups to share their dream jobs. She thinks this adaptation will help students think about more varied jobs in the real world. For Lesson 5, there is a reading passage about Simon's adventure in Kenya in the textbook. However, she worries that there are only simple activities to check students' understanding of the story. So, she will edit the story, intentionally deleting a few sentences at the end. This will challenge the students to think about the story's structure and look ahead to possible endings, using the storyline.

Based on <A>, identify the ONE objective that Ms. Lee wants to achieve through adaptation in Lesson 2 and the ONE objective in Lesson 5. Then, explain your answers with evidence from <A> and <B>.

First Draft

Revised Version

서술형 Worksheet

Topic/나의 점수/ 오답분석 및 채점기준	수정 전략 및 주제관련 정리(mapping)	Topic-related Key Terms & Concepts & Phrases
(1) Topic/나의 점수/정답률		
(2) Directions Analysis		
(3) Data Processing		

02 Read Mr. Han's materials for his level-differentiated classes, and follow the directions. [2 points] 2015 전공A 기입형 2번

The original text is for 2nd year high school students.

Original

No sooner had my plane landed than I was charmed by Korea. I particularly like the outdoor street markets and the strength and openness of the people who work there.

(A)

When my plane landed I was charmed by Korea. I particularly like the outdoor street markets and the strength and openness of the people there.

(B)

No sooner had my plane landed than I was enthralled by Korea. I particularly like the outdoor street markets and the integrity and receptiveness of the people who work there.

Complete the comments by filling in each blank with ONE word. Write your answers in the correct order.

> The original text has been adapted to suit the students' English proficiency levels. (A) shows how input is simplified through (1) _____ modification to make the original text easier for the lower level students. (B) shows how input is adapted through (2) _____ modification to make the original text more challenging for the upper level students.

Your Answer (1) _____

(2) _____

기입형 Worksheet

Topic/나의 점수/ 정답률	감점 원인 분석 및 수정전략	Topic-related Key Terms & Concepts & Phrases
	(1) 감점 원인 분석	
	(2) 수정 및 정리 전략 (mapping)	

03 Read the passages in <A> and <B>, and follow the directions. [4 points]

2022 전공A 12번

A

Digital technology provides students with a new battery of tools with which language can be learned effectively. Below are some apps that students can use for their English learning.

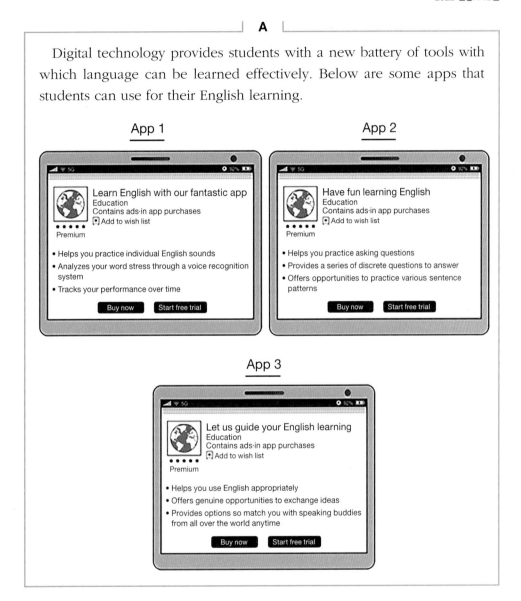

App 1

Learn English with our fantastic app
Education
Contains ads·in app purchases
⬆ Add to wish list
★ ★ ★ ★ ★
Premium

- Helps you practice individual English sounds
- Analyzes your word stress through a voice recognition system
- Tracks your performance over time

[Buy now] [Start free trial]

App 2

Have fun learning English
Education
Contains ads·in app purchases
⬆ Add to wish list
★ ★ ★ ★ ★
Premium

- Helps you practice asking questions
- Provides a series of discrete questions to answer
- Offers opportunities to practice various sentence patterns

[Buy now] [Start free trial]

App 3

Let us guide your English learning
Education
Contains ads·in app purchases
⬆ Add to wish list
★ ★ ★ ★ ★
Premium

- Helps you use English appropriately
- Offers genuine opportunities to exchange ideas
- Provides options so match you with speaking buddies from all over the world anytime

[Buy now] [Start free trial]

B

Minsu's Case

Minsu is very active in English classes and always looks for opportunities to speak English with other people. Since he lives in Korea, where English is not usually used outside the classroom, it is difficult to find English conversation partners. He once tried a conversation program where he spoke with native speakers on the phone. However, the program seemed too rigid in that he could only practice at designated times and with predetermined contents. Now, he wants to find an app where he can talk with partners whenever he wants and apply what he learns in the English class while speaking in a more natural context.

Jieun's Case

Jieun is afraid of speaking in English. But she was not like that before. She used to be outgoing and willing to communicate with people in English whenever she could. However, sometimes people didn't understand her and kept asking her to repeat the words she had just said. When she consulted her English teacher about the issue, the teacher advised her to focus on practicing pronunciation of words. Now, she is looking for an app which could help her practice pronouncing English words accurately.

Based on <A>, identify the ONE most appropriate English learning app for Minsu and Jieun, respectively. Then, explain your answers with evidence from <B>.

First Draft

_____

_____

_____

_____

_____

_____

_____

Revised Version

_____

_____

_____

_____

_____

_____

_____

서술형 Worksheet

Topic/나의 점수/ 오답분석 및 채점기준	수정 전략 및 주제관련 정리(mapping)	Topic-related Key Terms & Concepts & Phrases
(1) Topic/나의 점수/정답률		
(2) Directions Analysis		
(3) Data Processing		

Memo

Classroom Contexts

1 Learner Variables

01 kinesthetic

02 The students used three communication strategies: avoidance, appeal to authority, and word coinage. As corresponding evidence, first, the student avoids using the passive voice by not making 'bicycle' the subject. Second, the student appeals to authority by using a dictionary to find the synonym of 'make.' Finally, the students creates a non-existent word 'four-cycle,' instead of 'quadricycle.'

2 Classroom Management

01 Step 4 in <B> deviates from the suggestion of TBLT in <A> because the syllabus focuses mainly on teaching grammatical forms separately, rather than promoting communication.

02 In the lesson in <B>, students can achieve one oral language achievement standard, "talk about their worries and problems," by sharing their own worries and suggesting solutions in groups. They also meet one written language achievement standard, "read a short text about a familiar topic and organize the content," by completing a problem-solution chart after reading the text.

3 Textbook Evaluation and Adaptation, and Instruction Tools

01 Ms. Lee aims to encourage learners to tap into their own lives in Lesson 2 and enhance higher-level cognitive skills in Lesson 5. In Lesson 2, students discuss their dream jobs using magazine pictures of real-world occupations, helping them relate the content to their own lives and experiences. In Lesson 5, students predict or infer the missing ending of a story, which promotes higher-order thinking skills such as reasoning and interpretation.

02 (1) syntactic (2) lexical

03 App 3 is suitable for Minsu because it allows him to have real and natural conversations with speaking partners anytime, helping him use what he learns in a natural context. On the other hand, App 1 fits Jieun's needs, as it helps her improve her pronunciation by focusing on individual sounds and word stress, which is the main issue she struggles with.

Build Up

Chapter
03

Practical Language Teaching

Practical Language Teaching

>> 모범답안 p.106

1 Listening Skills

01 Read the passage in <A> and the sample items in <B>, and follow the directions. [4 points] 2021 전공B 9번

A

Ms. Kang, a new high school English teacher, was assigned to create questions for the listening section of the semester's final exam. In order to make the most effective test items, she goes over her notes from her college assessment class and finds the following:

> **<Item Techniques>**
>
> ✓ information transfer : transferring aural information to
> a visual representation
> ✓ partial dictation : writing down parts of what you hear
> while listening to a passage
> ✓ sentence paraphrase : choosing the correct paraphrase from
> 3-5 distractors
> ✓ sentence repetition : reproducing a stretch of aural language
> with oral repetition
> ✓ short answer : answering a question with a word or a short
> phrase without given choices

Looking at her notes, she remembers that each of these techniques has its own strengths. For example, the sentence paraphrase technique has high practicality because it is easy to grade. Other techniques, such as information transfer, partial dictation, and sentence repetition, work well for assessing students' listening ability in a more integrative way. Ms. Kang thinks that she will utilize some of these techniques because she wants to test her students' listening and other language skills simultaneously. Ms. Kang also thinks her students should be able to understand specific details, which is one of her main goals for the class this semester. So, she wants to test this particular ability in the final exam. While all the techniques in her notes are good for assessing the ability to find specific information, Ms. Kang thinks the sentence repetition technique may not be appropriate since it may only require students to simply repeat what they hear.

B

Below are two sample items made by Ms. Kang.

Sample Item 1

• Listen to the information about Minsu's daily schedule and fill in his schedule with the correct information. The information will be given twice.

Minsu's Schedule

	Monday	Tuesday	Wednesday	Thursday	Friday
9-10am					
10-11am					
11-12am					
12-1pm			Lunch		
1-2pm					
2-3pm					
3-4pm					

> ***Audio Script***
>
> Minsu's classes start at nine in the morning and he eats lunch at noon every day. He has math on Monday, Tuesday, and Friday at nine o'clock. English is scheduled on

Sample Item 2

• Fill in the blanks with the words you hear. You will hear the passage three times.

We can find many geographic regions in Korea. The _____ and _____ parts of the country have huge plains. The main rivers flow westward because the mountainous region is mostly on the _____ part of the country.

> *Audio Script*
>
> We can find many geographic regions in Korea. The southern and western parts of the country have huge plains. The main rivers flow westward because the mountainous region is mostly on the eastern part of the country.

Based on <A>, identify the item technique used in Sample Item 1 and Sample Item 2 in <B>, respectively. Then, explain why the teacher used both item techniques with evidence from <A>. Do NOT copy more than FOUR consecutive words from the passage.

First Draft

_____

_____

_____

_____

_____

_____

_____

Revised Version

_____

_____

_____

_____

_____

_____

_____

서술형 Worksheet

Topic/나의 점수/ 오답분석 및 채점기준	수정 전략 및 주제관련 정리(mapping)	Topic-related Key Terms & Concepts & Phrases
(1) Topic/나의 점수/정답률		
(2) Directions Analysis		
(3) Data Processing		

02 **Read the conversation and follow the directions.** [2 points] 2015 전공A 기입형 4번

T : The other day we were talking about the Battle of Waterloo. And we've already talked about the two main generals in that war. Does anybody remember who they are?

S1 : Napoleon and Wellington.

T : Correct, but don't forget that Wellington is a title which he received for his military successes. Born Arthur Wesley, he became the Duke of Wellington in 1814. He received that title for ending the Peninsular War by storming what city?

S2 : Toulouse.

T : That's right. Shortly after, Napoleon abdicated and was imprisoned on Elba. And when did the Battle of Waterloo take place?

S3 : 1815.

T : Very good. Napoleon escaped Elba and was attempting to restore his rule. It wasn't until his defeat at Waterloo by Wellington that Napoleon's reign finally came to an end. Now we're going to see...

T=teacher, S=student

Complete the comments on the conversation above by filling in the blank with ONE word.

The conversation above is part of a teacher-student talk in the classroom in which a teacher and students mainly give and receive specific information. Among types of speaking functions, the type shown in the conversation refers to situations where the focus is on information rather than on the participants. The conversation above serves a(n) _____ function in that its priority is not the interpersonal function of speaking but information exchange.

Your Answer _____

기입형 Worksheet

Topic/나의 점수/ 정답률	감점 원인 분석 및 수정전략	Topic-related Key Terms & Concepts & Phrases
	(1) 감점 원인 분석 (2) 수정 및 정리 전략 (mapping)	

2 Oral Skills

01 Read the activity procedure and identify the type of learning activity with ONE word. [2 points] 2016 전공A 3번

	Activity Procedure
Step 1	• T places various information on a different job in each of the four corners in the classroom. (Each corner is labelled with a different letter, A, B, C, or D.) • T assigns individual Ss a letter (A, B, C, or D) in order to create four groups of four Ss, each of which is a base group composed of A to D.
Step 2	• T provides Ss in each base group with handouts. (Each handout has a set of questions about four different jobs.) • T helps Ss understand that they should be interdependent upon one another not only for their own learning but also for the learning of others throughout the activity. • T informs Ss which corner to go to based on their letter in order to form four different expert groups.
Step 3	• Ss move to their expert groups and find out information about different jobs through discussions and answer the questions on the handouts. • T circulates within the groups and makes sure each of the Ss has all the answers.
Step 4	• Ss return to their initial base groups and exchange the information through discussing what they learned in the expert groups. • All the base groups present their findings to the whole class and decide which job they would like most.

T=teacher, S=student

Your Answer _____

기입형 Worksheet

Topic/나의 점수/ 정답률	감점 원인 분석 및 수정전략	Topic-related Key Terms & Concepts & Phrases
	(1) 감점 원인 분석 (2) 수정 및 정리 전략 (mapping)	

02 Read the passage in <A> and the conversation in <B>, and follow the directions. [4 points] 2016 전공A 12번

───────────┤ **A** ├───────────

Mr. Jeon's Thoughts

There are various types of teacher corrective feedback on learners' grammatical errors, including clarification request, elicitation, metalinguistic feedback and recast. I believe that corrective feedback may not have an immediate impact but it should meet certain requirements in order to facilitate language learning. I think corrective feedback should not explicitly indicate that an error has occurred so that it does not embarrass the learner inadvertently and disrupt the flow of ongoing communication. I also find it important that corrective feedback should contain a targetlike alternative to the learner's ill-formed output. Such an alternative form enables the learner to make a comparison of his or her problematic form and its correct form, which constitutes a cognitive process facilitative of language learning.

───────────┤ **B** ├───────────

S： I am very worried.
T： Really? What are you worried about, Minjae?
S： Math exam for tomorrow. I don't studied yesterday.
T： You didn't study yesterday?
S： No, I didn't studied.
T： Please tell me why. What happened?
S： I did volunteering all day long. So I don't had time to study.
T： Well, Minjae, "don't had" is not the right past tense form.
S： Uh, I didn't had time, time to study.

T=teacher, S=student

Identify the teacher's TWO corrective feedback utterances in <B> and select their respective type from those mentioned in <A>. Then explain how only ONE of the utterances meets what Mr. Jeon believes is required for effective corrective feedback in <A>.

First Draft

_____

_____

_____

_____

_____

_____

_____

Revised Version

_____

_____

_____

_____

_____

_____

_____

서술형 Worksheet

Topic/나의 점수/ 오답분석 및 채점기준	수정 전략 및 주제관련 정리(mapping)	Topic-related Key Terms & Concepts & Phrases
(1) Topic/나의 점수/정답률		
(2) Directions Analysis		
(3) Data Processing		

3 Reading Skills

01 **Read the passage and follow the directions.** [2 points] 2017 전공A 6번

> The following is part of a lesson procedure that aims to facilitate students' comprehension of a text concerning global warming.
>
> **Steps :**
> 1. Before reading the text, T activates Ss' background knowledge concerning global warming and provides other relevant information to help Ss to have a better comprehension of the text.
> 2. T instructs Ss to read the text quickly in order to grasp the main ideas. In doing so, T tells them not to read every word.
> 3. T asks Ss to reread it quickly for specific information, such as the type of disasters caused by global warming.
> 4. T instructs Ss to read the text again at their own pace.
> 5. T checks Ss' overall comprehension by having them write a brief summary of the text.
> 6. T then checks Ss' understanding of the details by using a cloze activity.
>
> T=teacher, S=student

Identify the two kinds of expeditious reading that the teacher instructs students to use in steps 2 and 3 with ONE word, respectively. Write them in the order that they appear.

(Your Answer) _____

기입형 Worksheet

Topic/나의 점수/ 정답률	감점 원인 분석 및 수정전략	Topic-related Key Terms & Concepts & Phrases
	(1) 감점 원인 분석	
	(2) 수정 및 정리 전략 (mapping)	

02 Read the conversation between two high school English teachers, and identify the type of reading that Ms. Kim recommends to Mr. Hong. Use **TWO words.** [2 points] 2015 전공A 기입형 5번

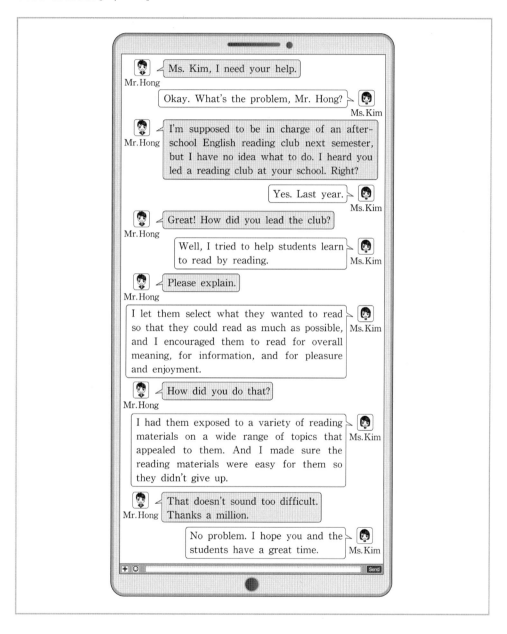

Your Answer _____

기입형 Worksheet

Topic/나의 점수/ 정답률	감점 원인 분석 및 수정전략	Topic-related Key Terms & Concepts & Phrases
	(1) 감점 원인 분석 (2) 수정 및 정리 전략 (mapping)	

4 Writing Skills

01 Read the lesson procedure and complete the objectives by filling in each blank with TWO words. Write your answers in the correct order. [2 points]

2014 전공A 기입형 9번

Students : 2nd year middle school students
Approximate time : 45 minutes
Lesson objectives :

Students will be able :
- to describe a daily routine using correct verb forms and (1) _____ from a sample paragraph
- to revise writing through (2) _____ on first drafts

- -

Lesson Procedure

1. The teacher asks students what they do when they get home every day.
2. Students take turns asking and answering questions about their daily routine in pairs. Students take notes on each other's answers.
3. The teacher provides a sample paragraph, and students choose the correct expressions.

> (As soon as/Since) Taebin finishes school, he goes to taekwondo. When he arrives, he puts on his workout clothes, and (first/then) he practices. (After/Before) he finishes, he rides his bike home. (As soon as/After that), he takes a shower. (After/Next), he eats his dinner. (Before/When) he finishes dinner, he does his homework. (Before/While) he goes to bed, he brushes his teeth.

4. Students use their notes to write a short paragraph about their partner's daily routine.
5. Students exchange writings and underline their partner's mistakes using the checklist.
   - Are the present forms of verbs used correctly?
   - Are the events described in time order?
   - Is time order indicated using the expressions focused upon in the sample paragraph?
   - Is punctuation used correctly?
6. Students rewrite their paragraph based on Step 5.

Your Answer (1) _____

(2) _____

기입형 Worksheet

Topic/나의 점수/ 정답률	감점 원인 분석 및 수정전략	Topic-related Key Terms & Concepts & Phrases
	(1) 감점 원인 분석 (2) 수정 및 정리 전략 (mapping)	

02 Read the teacher's reflection and follow the directions. [4 points] 2021 전공B 6번

Teacher's Reflection

This semester I have been using a checklist in my English writing class to help my students revise their drafts by themselves. The checklist I provide for my students covers the following areas: content, organization, grammar, vocabulary, and mechanics. Below is a part of the checklist.

Areas	Indicators	Yes	No
(1) _____	I use correct subject and verb agreement.		
	I use verb tense correctly.		
(2) _____	I put a period at the end of every sentence.		
	I use capital letters correctly.		
	I spell the words correctly.		

At first, the checklist didn't seem feasible because there was little improvement, especially in organization in writing. To find the reason, I held group conferences with the students and discovered that the indicators for organization were too complicated for them to understand. Some of them included more than one aspect to check simultaneously. So, I divided those indicators into two or three separate sentences so that one indicator assesses only one aspect. Since the revision of the indicators, the students' organization has gotten much better.

However, some students still had problems using the checklist appropriately. So, I ran a couple of training sessions to teach the students what the indicators meant and how they should be utilized. First, we read the indicators and I asked if they made sense. Then, I had them practice checking particular errors with a sample paragraph I had prepared. Since the training sessions, the students have been making significantly fewer errors. Overall, the use of the checklist has worked well in the revision process.

Fill in the blanks (1) and (2) with the ONE most appropriate word from the teacher's reflection, respectively. Then, explain how the teacher solved the problems encountered while using the checklist. Do NOT copy more than FIVE consecutive words from the passage.

First Draft

_____

_____

_____

_____

_____

_____

_____

Revised Version

_____

_____

_____

_____

_____

_____

_____

서술형 Worksheet

Topic/나의 점수/ 오답분석 및 채점기준	수정 전략 및 주제관련 정리(mapping)	Topic-related Key Terms & Concepts & Phrases
(1) Topic/나의 점수/정답률		
(2) Directions Analysis		
(3) Data Processing		

5 Vocabulary & Grammar Teaching

01 **Read the conversation and follow the directions.** [2 points] 2024 전공A 2번

> T1: Hi, Mr. Lee. What are you reading?
>
> T2: Oh, hello. It's a book about the role of input in language acquisition. It's quite fascinating.
>
> T1: What does it say?
>
> T2: Well, it introduces some empirical studies on the effects of _____ in language development.
>
> T1: Oh, I think I heard that term before. Can you remind me?
>
> T2: The term is defined as how prominent or easy a certain input is to hear or read compared to other features around it.
>
> T1: I see. So, it means the ability of a stimulus to stand out from the rest of the input.
>
> T2: Exactly. Some features that are more prominent or easier may be more noticeable and will attract attention from learners.
>
> T1: During classroom interaction, I always try to highlight the keywords or phrases in various ways, and it means that I've been doing things correctly.
>
> T2: Yeah, you're doing great. This book also says teachers need to increase the frequency of exposure because when students encounter certain words and phrases more often, they tend to notice them more effectively.
>
> T1: I understand. I guess it's also because of the functions of salience.
>
> T2: You're right. The more frequently specific vocabulary and grammatical patterns appear, the more likely they facilitate noticing and detection. So, it's not just about teaching a wide range of vocabulary and complex grammar rules but also ensuring students encounter them regularly.
>
> T1: Sounds good to me.
>
> T=teacher

Fill in the blank with the ONE most appropriate word from the conversation.

Your Answer _____

기입형 Worksheet

Topic/나의 점수/ 정답률	감점 원인 분석 및 수정전략	Topic-related Key Terms & Concepts & Phrases
	(1) 감점 원인 분석 (2) 수정 및 정리 전략 (mapping)	

02 Read the passage in <A> and the teaching procedures in <B>, and follow the directions. [4 points] 2023 전공B 10번

A

The basic aspects the students need to know about a lexical item are its written and spoken forms, and its denotational meaning. However, there are additional aspects which also need to be learned, as are described in the following table.

Aspects	Descriptions
Grammar	A grammatical structure may be lexically bound, and lexical items also have grammatical features.
Collocation	Collocation refers to the way words tend to co-occur with other words or expressions.
Connotation	The connotations of a word are the emotional or positive-negative associations that it implies.
Appropriateness	Students need to know if a particular lexical item is usually used in writing or in speech; or in formal or informal discourse.
Word formation	Words can be broken down into morphemes. Exactly how these components are put together is another piece of useful information.

B

Teaching Procedure 1

1. Present the following expressions in the table. Ask students to choose which expressions are possible.

do my homework	(O/X)	make my homework	(O/X)
do some coffee	(O/X)	make some coffee	(O/X)
do the laundry	(O/X)	make the laundry	(O/X)

2. Ask students to find more examples using *do* and *make*, referencing an online concordancer.

Teaching Procedure 2

1. Ask students to identify countable and uncountable nouns.

advice	employee	equipment	facility
information	money	proposal	result

2. Tell students to choose the expression of quantity that does NOT fit with the noun in each sentence.

(a) The researchers found [*a significant proportion of / some of / most of*] the results were not corroborated by other sources.

Identify ONE aspect in <A> that each teaching procedure in <B> focuses on, respectively. Then, explain your answers with evidence from <B>.

First Draft

_____

_____

_____

_____

_____

_____

_____

Revised Version

_____

_____

_____

_____

_____

_____

_____

서술형 Worksheet

Topic/나의 점수/ 오답분석 및 채점기준	수정 전략 및 주제관련 정리(mapping)	Topic-related Key Terms & Concepts & Phrases
(1) Topic/나의 점수/정답률		
(2) Directions Analysis		
(3) Data Processing		

03 Read the passage in <A> and the master plan in <B>, and follow the directions. [4 points] 2025 전공B 11번

A

Ms. Kim, a high school English teacher, attended an ICT workshop for English teachers. There she learned how to select digital tools that best fit her students' needs and use them appropriately. Below is the list of principles she took note of during the workshop.

⟨Guiding principles for using digital tools⟩

① Encourage students to independently explore and discover language rules.

② Support learners with diverse learning styles (e.g., auditory styles, visual styles).

③ Teach digital ethics (e.g., citing properly).

④ Assess student achievement and provide individualized feedback.

B

Draft of the Master Plan

Unit	Save the Earth	
Objectives	Students will be able to: • identify the main idea and details of a text or discourse • write an opinion using textual and non-textual elements • use digital tools responsibly and ethically	
Period	**Contents**	**Technology**
1st	• Introduce the topic, 'Save the Earth' • Watch a video on environmental problems • Teach how to use the Internet properly (e.g., locating information, sourcing, netiquette)	- Online videos - Internet search engines
2nd	• Make predictions about a text using titles and pictures • Read the passage, 'Plastic Pollution' • Identify key words and main ideas	- Word cloud generator to visualize key concepts
3rd	• Provide definitions of new words • Teach grammar points explicitly using drills	- PPT slides
…	…	…
7th	• Brainstorm ideas to solve environmental problems and share in groups • In groups, create a 'Save the Earth' poster	- Online collaborative writing platform
8th	• Exhibit groups' posters on the walls • Conduct a team-based quiz and provide comments to groups	- Online quiz platform

Based on <A>, identify the TWO guiding principles that Ms. Kim does NOT conform to in her lessons in <B>. Then, explain your answers, respectively, with evidence from <B>.

First Draft

_____

_____

_____

_____

_____

_____

_____

_____

Revised Version

_____

_____

_____

_____

_____

_____

_____

_____

서술형 Worksheet

Topic/나의 점수/ 오답분석 및 채점기준	수정 전략 및 주제관련 정리(mapping)	Topic-related Key Terms & Concepts & Phrases
(1) Topic/나의 점수/정답률		
(2) Directions Analysis		
(3) Data Processing		

04 Read Ms. Lee's opinions about the grammar lesson in <A> and the sample lesson plan in <B>, and follow the directions. [4 points] 2018 전공B 5번

A

I think teachers should keep in mind that the ultimate goal of any grammar lesson is to build up communicative ability. In order to achieve this goal, I believe that classroom activities should not focus on practicing structures and patterns in a meaningless way. Instead, they should be designed to involve students in real communication. By doing so, grammar lessons will be able to encourage the students' interest in learning and elicit more active and meaningful interaction with others in the classroom.

B

Subject	High School English		Students	1st-year students
Title	Lesson 9 My Dream		Date	Nov. 24th
Objectives	• Students will familiarize themselves with the expression "If I were ... ." • Students will be able to communicate using the expression "If I were ... ."			
Teaching-Learning Activities				
Introduction	Greeting & Roll-call	• T and Ss exchange greetings. • T checks if all the Ss are present.		
	Review	• T reviews materials from the previous lesson.		
	Stating the Objectives	• T introduces the objective of the lesson.		
Development	Activity 1	• T hands out a text that contains several instances of "If I were ... ." • Ss scan the text and highlight all the sentences including "If I were ... ." • Ss check the ones they highlighted with T. • T tells Ss to pay attention to the verb form "were."		

	Activity 2	• T tells Ss that she is going to read a passage on "My Dream." • T explains difficult words in the passage. • T reads the passage at a normal pace. • Ss jot down the key words in the passage as T reads. • Ss reconstruct the passage individually. • T hands out the original text to Ss.
	Activity 3	• T has Ss form groups of three. • T asks Ss to think of a job that they would like to have in the future. • Ss use "If I were … " to share their opinions about their future dream jobs. • Assuming that their dreams come true, two Ss take a reporter's role and interview the other S asking how he or she feels about his or her job. • Ss take turns and continue the activity.
	Activity 4	• T hands out a worksheet. • Ss put together sentence fragments to form complete sentences. • T reads out complete sentences and each S checks their own answers. • T writes three more sentences using "If I were … " on the board. • T asks Ss to read the sentences.
Consolidation	Review	• T reviews what Ss learned.
	Closure	• T hands out homework and announces the next lesson. • T says goodbye to Ss.

T=teacher, S=student

Based on <A>, choose the ONE most appropriate activity in the development stage that reflects Ms. Lee's opinions. Then, support your choice with evidence from <B>. Do NOT copy more than FOUR consecutive words from the passage.

First Draft

_____

_____

_____

_____

_____

_____

_____

Revised Version

_____

_____

_____

_____

_____

_____

_____

서술형 Worksheet

Topic/나의 점수/ 오답분석 및 채점기준	수정 전략 및 주제관련 정리(mapping)	Topic-related Key Terms & Concepts & Phrases
(1) Topic/나의 점수/정답률		
(2) Directions Analysis		
(3) Data Processing		

Memo

1 Listening Skills

01 Ms. Kang uses 'information transfer' and 'partial dictation' in Sample Item 1 and 2, respectively. Through these techniques, she aims to assess students' listening skills in combination with other skills in an integrative ways. Also, she wants to assess students' ability to find specific details while listening.

02 transactional

2 Oral Skills

01 jigsaw

02 The teacher used recast by saying, "You didn't study yesterday?" and metalinguistic feedback by saying, "'don't had' is not the right past tense form." According to Mr. Jeon, recast is more effective because it does not explicitly point out the error and maintains the flow of communication while offering a target-like form.

3 Reading Skills

01 skimming, scanning

02 extensive reading

4 Writing Skills

01 (1) time order (2) peer editing

02 (1) Grammar (2) Mechanics
When the checklist was not feasible, the teacher provided two solutions. First, she/he revised the complicated organization indicators into several simplified sentences so that each assessed a single aspect. Then, through training session, she/he helped students understand the indicators and practice how to use them properly.

5 Vocabulary & Grammar Teaching

01 salience

02 Teaching Procedures 1 and 2 focus on collocation and grammar, respectively. The former helps students identify acceptable word combinations by presenting expressions that commonly co-occur with "do" and "make." The latter asks students to distinguish countable and uncountable nouns and select appropriate expressions of quantity.

03 Ms. Kim does not conform to guiding principles ① and ④. First, she explicitly teaches grammar points through drills instead of encouraging students to independently explore and discover language rules. Additionally, she conducts a team-based quiz and provides comments to groups rather than assessing individual performance and offering personalized feedback.

04 Activity 3 best reflects Ms. Lee's opinion about how a grammar lesson should be taught. In this activity, students use the target phrase "If I were..." by exchanging their future job ideas in groups. Through paired interviews, they engage in active and meaningful interaction, which aligns with Ms. Lee's view that grammar activities should promote real communication.

Build Up

Chapter
04

Classroom Assessment

Chapter 04

Classroom Assessment

≫ 모범답안 p.130

1 Assessment Principles

01 Read the conversation in \<A\> and the passage in \<B\>, and follow the directions. [2 points] 2025 전공A 4번

A

(Two teachers, Mr. Lee and Ms. Kim, recently scored students' speaking assessments. They later discussed the scoring process and Mr. Lee reflected on his scoring experiences in his journals.)

Mr. Lee : As I was reviewing my ratings, I noticed that they were staying consistent throughout the scoring process.

Ms. Kim : Good, it's actually hard to keep the same perspective when grading multiple students. But you mean you found actual similarities in your scores for the same students over time?

Mr. Lee : Yes, exactly. I think I might have benefitted from reviewing my previous scores before re-evaluating anyone's performance to see if I'm staying consistent.

Ms. Kim : That makes sense. You know, I've noticed that we have some scoring differences between us on certain criteria.

Mr. Lee : Right. I normally give a score of 10 if students have natural flow even though they may demonstrate some errors in grammar or vocabulary. How about you?

Ms. Kim : Oh, I've constantly made efforts to adhere to our scoring criteria, and I give a perfect score only when they speak without any errors or hesitation.

Mr. Lee : All right. Now I can see why we have different scoring results and it makes me think—these different results could send mixed messages to students.

Ms. Kim : I agree. Let's review our criteria and stick to following our rubric.

Mr. Lee : Sure. That would be fairer for the students.

B

Mr. Lee's Reflective Journal

After today's grading session, I reviewed my scores and luckily noticed consistency in my ratings for the same students across different sessions. However, after talking with Ms. Kim, I realized that we provided different scores for the same students. I'm concerned this could lead to some confusion if they receive different scores based on which teacher assesses them. I think it would be helpful if Ms. Kim and I could go over the rubric together to ensure a more unified scoring approach.

04

Fill in the blanks with the TWO most appropriate words.

Based on <A> and <B>, Mr. Lee is concerned about the lack of _____ _____ in the scoring process. His concern is not about the consistency of rating by a single rater but about the consistency of rating by different raters.

Your Answer

기입형 Worksheet

Topic/나의 점수/ 정답률	감점 원인 분석 및 수정전략	Topic-related Key Terms & Concepts & Phrases
	(1) 감점 원인 분석 (2) 수정 및 정리 전략 (mapping)	

02 Read the passage in <A> and the teacher's reflection log in <B>, and follow the directions. [4 points] 2025 전공A 9번

A

　　Mr. Jeong, an English teacher, was tasked with evaluating speaking assessment items in his students' final exam. Reviewing key principles of speaking assessment, he noted the following:

　✓ Clarity: Prompts should be straightforward to avoid confusion.
　✓ Authenticity: Speaking tasks should mirror real-life communication, enabling students to demonstrate natural language use.
　✓ Integrated Skills Assessment: Tasks should assess speaking alongside other skills, such as listening comprehension, to reflect communicative performance.
　✓ Practicality: Test items should be feasible and manageable in terms of the time spent in assessment.

B

Teacher's Reflection Log

　　After reviewing the items, I felt that the two items had some good and bad points. Item 1 asked students to describe a memorable experience that they had with a friend, including details such as when it happened, what they did, and why it was memorable. After observing students' responses, I realized that this item resembled a conversation topic in real-life contexts. However, I regret that I didn't set time limits for the item and it took too much time to score it, which made the assessment difficult to manage.

　　For Item 2, after looking at a picture of a busy street, students were asked to describe what they saw. Most of the students did very well on this task because the item clearly described what sort of response was desired. I think this item was effective in assessing pronunciation, one of the criteria for assessing speaking skills. However, next time I want to add some more items such as asking students to listen to a short audio and discuss their opinions. It might be more challenging but I believe I can assess multiple skills in the test.

Based on <A>, identify the speaking assessment principles applied in Item 1 and Item 2 in <B>, respectively. Then, explain how each principle was applied in each item with evidence from <B>.

First Draft

Revised Version

서술형 Worksheet

Topic/나의 점수/ 오답분석 및 채점기준	수정 전략 및 주제관련 정리(mapping)	Topic-related Key Terms & Concepts & Phrases
(1) Topic/나의 점수/정답률		
(2) Directions Analysis		
(3) Data Processing		

04

03 **Examine part of a test evaluation checklist by a head teacher and a student's reflective journal about the test, and follow the directions.**
[4 points] 2016 전공A 13번

Mr. Kim, a head teacher of high school English, wanted to evaluate the achievement test of English reading in order to find to what extent the five major principles of language assessment (practicality, reliability, validity, authenticity, and washback) were applied to the test.

TEST EVALUATION CHECKLIST

Test-takers: 2nd year high school students

Content	Scale		
	1	2	3
Subjectivity does not enter into the scoring process.	☐	☐	■
Classroom conditions for the test are equal for all students.	☐	☐	■
Test measures exactly what it is supposed to measure.	■	☐	☐
Items focus on previously practiced in-class reading skills.	■	☐	☐
Topics and situations are interesting.	☐	☐	■
Tasks replicate, or closely approximate, real-world tasks.	☐	☐	■

1=poor, 2=average, 3=good

Post-Exam Reflection

I studied really hard for the test because I wanted to move to a higher level class. But I got 76 and I was so disappointed. Since there were no errors in scoring, my score was dependable, I think. The topics were very relevant to my real life. But what was the problem? Did I use the wrong study skills? Actually I was very surprised when I first saw the test. Lots of tasks were very unfamiliar and I believe I've never done those kinds of tasks in class. Furthermore, after the test I actually expected the teacher to go over the test and give advice on what I should focus on in the future. It never happened. No feedback or comments from the teacher were given. I was not sure which items I got wrong. I will have the same type of test next semester and I'm not sure how I can improve my reading skills and get a better grade.

04

Identify TWO well-applied principles and TWO poorly-applied principles among the five principles of language assessment stated above based on all the data. Then support each of your choices with details from the post-exam reflection ONLY.

First Draft

Revised Version

서술형 Worksheet

Topic/나의 점수/ 오답분석 및 채점기준	수정 전략 및 주제관련 정리(mapping)	Topic-related Key Terms & Concepts & Phrases
(1) Topic/나의 점수/정답률		
(2) Directions Analysis		
(3) Data Processing		

2   Multiple-choice Item Testing

01   **Read the passage and follow the directions.** [2 points] 2015 전공A 기입형 3번

Mr. Lee's English listening test consisted exclusively of four-option, multiple-choice items. After scoring the test, he calculated the response frequency for each item. Part of the results is presented below.

Item \ Option	Upper Group (N=100)				Lower Group (N=100)			
	A	B	C	D	A	B	C	D
1	50%*	27%	13%	10%	10%*	45%	25%	20%
2	13%	10%	70%*	7%	25%	27%	28%*	20%
3	20%	25%	18%	37%*	21%	26%	16%	37%*
...								
17	4%	0%	61%	35%*	66%	0%	29%	5%*
...								

* indicates the correct response.

Complete the comments on item analysis by filling in each blank with ONE word. Write your answers in the correct order.

Items 1 and 2 seem to be fulfilling their function. Item 3 has the problem of item (1) _____. Therefore, option D of item 3 needs to be revised or item 3 needs to be discarded. Item 17 has a problem with its (2) _____: No one from the upper group and lower group chose option B, and many upper group students incorrectly chose option C.

Your Answer (1) _____

(2) _____

기입형 Worksheet

Topic/나의 점수/ 정답률	감점 원인 분석 및 수정전략	Topic-related Key Terms & Concepts & Phrases
	(1) 감점 원인 분석	
	(2) 수정 및 정리 전략 (mapping)	

02 **Read the passage and follow the directions.** [2 points] 2023 전공A 4번

A test taker is sitting in front of a computer, examining some sample items, and quickly learns how to take computer-based tests. Meanwhile, a computer program begins to 'guess' his ability level, and keeps trying to 'match' the test with his current language ability. This is how this technique works.

The computer program usually begins by showing an item of moderate difficulty, for example, an item that the test taker has a fifty percent chance of getting right. If he gets this item right, the computer program reestimates his ability level in real time and shows either an item of equal difficulty or a slightly more challenging item. If the test taker gets his first item wrong, however, the computer program will show either an item of equal or slightly lesser difficulty. The test taker keeps taking the test until, for instance, he gets several items wrong in a row. To put it another way, the computer program repeats its matching work until it collects enough information to determine the test taker's current English ability level.

Fill in the blank with the THREE most appropriate words.

The testing procedure described above enables us to make more individualized and educationally useful tests. It can also provide test takers with a better test-taking experience with fewer items, and with increased precision. This testing procedure is commonly referred to as _____.

Your Answer _____

기입형 Worksheet

Topic/나의 점수/ 정답률	감점 원인 분석 및 수정전략	Topic-related Key Terms & Concepts & Phrases
	(1) 감점 원인 분석 (2) 수정 및 정리 전략 (mapping)	

3 Performance-based Testing

01 Read the English test task specifications in <A> and the teacher's reflective journal in <B>, and follow the directions. [4 points] 2019 전공A 12번

A

Test Task Specifications

Category	Description
Purpose	To determine students' current levels and place them into the most appropriate speaking courses
Time allocation	2 minutes (1 minute for preparation and 1 minute for speaking)
Task type	Picture-cued tasks
Scoring method	Analytic a. Criteria: Content, Fluency, Accuracy, Pronunciation b. Each criterion is worth 5 points and the score for this task is added up to 20.
Scoring procedure	a. Two examiners: a primary examiner who conducts the test and a secondary examiner who observes the test b. If there is a difference of more than 2 points in total, the examiners discuss rating disagreements based on the recorded test to arrive at a rating that they agree upon.

B

I understand that some students have potential strengths in learning languages, and in order to check my students' aptitude in English, I conducted a speaking test with picture-cued tasks. For each task, students looked at pictures and prepared for 1 minute and then described them for 1 minute. I found that 1 minute was not enough for my students to prepare their answers, so I felt that I needed to change the time allocation for the task. In addition, although my rating and the other examiner's rating seemed consistent, I realized that my approach, providing a global rating with overall impressions using a single general scale, was not very effective because the scores didn't give much helpful information to students. ... There was one student's test yielding very different scores, so we (primary and secondary examiners) had a discussion about the recorded test and found that I gave the wrong score by mistake. It was good that we recorded the test even though both of us were present during the test.

Identify TWO categories that the teacher did NOT follow in the test task specifications from <A>. Then, support your answers with evidence from <B>.

First Draft

_____

_____

_____

_____

Revised Version

_____

_____

_____

_____

서술형 Worksheet

Topic/나의 점수/ 오답분석 및 채점기준	수정 전략 및 주제관련 정리(mapping)	Topic-related Key Terms & Concepts & Phrases
(1) Topic/나의 점수/정답률		
(2) Directions Analysis		
(3) Data Processing		

02 **Read the dialogue and follow the directions.** [4 points] 2018 전공A 13번

T : Come here, Sumin. How was your vacation?

S : Pretty good. Thank you, Ms. Kim. Actually, I'm so happy to be taking English classes from you this year.

T : Good! You're really welcome in my class. Okay, then, let's talk about the test you had.

S : You mean the reading test you gave us in the first class? Actually, I was wondering why you gave us a test instead of going directly into the textbook.

T : Right, your class hasn't had a lesson yet. It was mainly to see how much you are ready for this semester and give you individual attention for any strong and weak points you have.

S : I see. So, how were the results?

T : Hmm... Overall, you did quite well. Especially, you did well on the grammar questions. But it appears you had a bit of trouble with some words in the reading texts.

S : You're right. Some words are really hard to memorize although I keep trying.

T : I understand. Well, why don't you try to learn them through a context particularly relevant to you? That will be helpful, I believe.

S : Thank you for your advice, Ms. Kim.

T=teacher, S=student

Fill in the blank with the ONE most appropriate word. Then, support your answer with evidence from the dialogue.

> Tests can be categorized according to the purposes for which they are carried out. In this respect, the test that Ms. Kim and Sumin are talking about is an example of a(n) _____ test.

First Draft

_____

_____

_____

_____

_____

_____

_____

Revised Version

_____

_____

_____

_____

_____

_____

_____

서술형 Worksheet

Topic/나의 점수/ 오답분석 및 채점기준	수정 전략 및 주제관련 정리(mapping)	Topic-related Key Terms & Concepts & Phrases
(1) Topic/나의 점수/정답률		
(2) Directions Analysis		
(3) Data Processing		

Memo

Classroom Assessment

본문 p.110

1 Assessment Principles

01 inter-rater reliability

02 Authenticity is applied to Item 1 because the conversation topic about memorable experience with friends reflects real-life contexts. On the other hand, Clarity is applied to Item 2, because the use of a prompt, 'a picture of a busy street', enables students to clearly describe what they observed.

03 According to the data, this test has high reliability and authenticity. This shows that the scoring is reliable and fair, and the topics are relevant to students' real lives. However, it lacks validity and washback. This is because the test includes tasks that students have never done in class. Moreover, the student received no comments or feedback on the results to help improve further.

2 Multiple-choice Item Testing

01 (1) discrimination (2) distractors

02 computer adaptive testing / computerized adaptive testing

3 Performance-based Testing

01 The teacher in <B> does not follow two test task specifications from <A>: Purpose and Scoring method. Specifically, the teacher conducts the test to check students' aptitude (potential strength) in English, rather than to place them into the appropriate level speaking course. Also, instead of using an analytic scoring method, the teacher uses a holistic rating with one general scale.

02 diagnostic

The test is designed to diagnose the student's readiness for the upcoming semester and identify her strengths and weaknesses. As a result, it reveals that she had acquired grammatical knowledge well but lacked vocabulary knowledge.

NEW

Build Up

박현수 영어교육론 Ⅲ-2 기출문제

Guideline for Pre-service Teachers

나의 기출분석 및 오답분석

초판인쇄 | 2025. 5. 2. **초판발행** | 2025. 5. 9. **편저자** | 박현수
발행인 | 박 용 **발행처** | (주)박문각출판 **표지디자인** | 박문각 디자인팀
등록 | 2015년 4월 29일 제2019-000137호
주소 | 06654 서울시 서초구 효령로 283 서경빌딩 **팩스** | (02)584-2927
전화 | 교재주문·학습문의 (02)6466-7202

정가 27,000원(1, 2권 포함)
ISBN 979-11-7262-794-2 | ISBN 979-11-7262-792-8(세트)